Covenant *Dating*

The Companion
Study Guide For
Covenant Dating
The Biblical Path
to Marriage

Beverly D. Allen
Dr. Stephaine Arrington

WESTBOW
PRESS®
A DIVISION OF THOMAS NELSON
& ZONDERVAN

WestBow Press books may be ordered through booksellers or by contacting:

WestBow Press
A Division of Thomas Nelson & Zondervan
1663 Liberty Drive
Bloomington, IN 47403
www.westbowpress.com
844-714-3454

Scripture is quoted from the King James Version of the Bible.

ISBN: 978-1-6642-1173-5 (sc)
ISBN: 978-1-6642-1172-8 (e)

Print information available on the last page.

WestBow Press rev. date: 12/07/2020

Acknowledgments

It gives me such great pleasure to acknowledge and give personal thanks to my dear Sister Friend for over ten years—and proven saint and loving, trustworthy Sister—Dr. Stephaine Arrington. She is regal, a Queen serving the Lord in integrity and obedience with love for God's people. I love this dear Sister Gurl dearly and admire her along with all her accomplishments, academically as well as spiritually. She has humility with confidence in who she is and what the Lord has blessed her with, and no signs of arrogance.

I am thankful to the Lord for His leading to inviting her to co-author my companion study guide and teaching tool to help absorb and retain the message of my book *Covenant Dating: The Biblical Path to Marriage*. From the time I presented the idea to Stephaine, she has been nothing but committed, dedicated, and focused on completing this project in a timely manner.

As a college professor for many years, Stephaine knows the most stimulating ways to teach subjects and engage readers, which is what I needed to be done. Stephaine has aided me tremendously in sculpting and designing a presentation to help believers in the body of Christ honor God's mandate for meaningful relationships according to His plan and not the newest and latest dictates of the world or contemporary society. The enemy has crept in "unawares" and weakened many believers to accept worldly lusts, forfeiting the struggle against gratifying the flesh, which will never bring true peace, joy, and righteousness, nor promote holiness unto the Lord.

I would not have been able to complete this project in the manner it has been done without the cooperation and camaraderie Stephaine and I was able to experience. To say thank you is too trivial; to say congratulations on your first author experience is long overdue. I know that this is just the beginning of a new path as an author, with many more to come. Stephaine, my Sister, thank you for saying yes and being obedient to the voice of the Lord. I love you to eternity and have gratitude and great appreciation for your consistent friendship, which has never wavered.

Finally, I would like to also acknowledge another individual who makes me look good every time he clicks the camera in my direction. A young man I refer to as "Nephew", Brother Matthew Dennis, who is a gifted and anointed photographer. Thank you Matthew for taking the beautiful picture that I have affixed on the back cover of this workbook. I am so proud of your work and wanted to display it to the world.

My admiration, reverence, and love for Evangelist Beverly Allen continue to forestall any perception of boundaries as she has afforded me yet another opportunity to be a participant in her presentation of wisdom and guidance concerning God's divine relationship with humanity. Her profound understanding of biblical precepts provokes any listener or reader to easily be engaged in the multitude of concepts of which she can expertly speak or write. It is because of her unyielding faith and willing obedience that my testimony of God's plan for my life is elevated. She is a consummate preacher, teacher, and mentor extraordinaire.

Over the past twenty years or more, Evangelist Allen and I have had multiple instances to work on projects together and each has had a tremendous impact on my professional, personal, and spiritual development. We have lovingly embraced varied celebrations of life encompassing laughter and tears too numerous to mention. Subsequently, however, as we have pursued collaborative and independent initiatives designed to please the Lord, I gratefully acknowledge the enormity that this project represents. Although words could hardly express my intense delight, enthusiasm, and privilege in being chosen to write the Preface in Evangelist Allen's book titled *Good Women in Bad Situations and the Grace That Awaits Them* in 2009; I'm truly now blessed beyond measure to have been afforded this occasion to co-author our current work *Covenant Dating: The Biblical Path to Marriage - Transformative Tool and Companion Study Guide for Groups or Individuals.*

Because of God's unmerited favor, the publication of this book attests to God's infallible word recorded in Philippians 1: 3-6 and upon which this acknowledgment rests:

I thank my God upon every remembrance of you,
Always in every prayer of mine for you all making request with joy,
For your fellowship in the gospel from the first day until now;
Being confident of this very thing, that he which hath begun a good work in you
will perform it until the day of Jesus Christ…

My heart is overwhelmed with magnanimous appreciation and humility for Evangelist Beverly Allen's predilection to share this sacred treasure, and allowing me to partner with her in this comprehensive and significant endeavor. Thank you *My Sistah, My Friend,* again and again and again for this platform to share your gift with others.

Finally, special thanks to my eldest son Daryl whose technical assistance was immeasurable! I love you to the moon and back.

Dear Heavenly Father

Help me to see who I am in You, that I might recognize and become in conduct and lifestyle the son/daughter You died for and cleansed me to be. As a new creature in Christ, help me to be aware of the power within me to live holy and righteous in this present world and bring You glory and honor. Build within me a hunger and thirst for Your Word so that I might read and retain it in my heart and not sin against You.

I present my body to You as a living sacrifice and confess that I am not my own, for I have been bought with a price—by the precious blood of Jesus Christ, my Lord and my God! My body is the temple of the living God, and I reserve it for You and my covenant partner when and if You send that person to me. Until that time, I commit my body, my emotions, and my will to You and Your Word. I make Your will more important than my will and ask for it to be done. In Your strength, I will wait on You patiently and work to build up the kingdom of God and be a living witness to others of Your love, mercy, and grace.

No Man's Concubine
Evangelist Beverly D. Allen

Table of Contents

Introduction

Dating is not meant to be casual and when undertaken properly focuses on achieving a covenant relationship. So the goal of dating for those in the kingdom of God is to seek and pursue a potential covenant partner while adhering to biblical guidance and obedience toward a path to marriage. True joy comes from obedience to God and His Word, which is meant to protect your heart, your emotions, and above all your spiritual relationship with God, our Father. Yes, God rewards and honors obedience.

A covenant relationship is the most sacred of relationships. We are passionately involved in helping to promote change within individual believers professing salvation through Jesus Christ, how they view marriage in light of God's divine covenant plan. Although many people believe that the rate of divorce is higher in Christian culture than other religious cultures, there is not substantial evidence to support this premise. Nonetheless, we can only say that outside of abuse, adultery, and abandonment; marriage was to be irrevocable and could only be separated by death. Consequently, many well-intentioned couples are not informed, taught, or counseled on what God had in mind when He established a covenantal relationship with man and what it continues to represent today.

According to Ephesians 5:28-33, the first bride and bridegroom of creation typified the bride and bridegroom of redemption, Christ and His Church (Conner and Malmin 15). It is with this understanding that this companion workbook was developed to help teach and motivate as well as to encourage the process of dating and courtship leading to marriage. With this in mind, particularly believers or anyone not serving Jesus Christ to know what God requires and what man must take into consideration when preparing the marital vows, they are about to make toward one another.

This workbook is an excellent resource for group studies as well as individuals who are contemplating entering into relationships that they may have a guide of how to navigate within the boundaries of Scripture. Get ready for the exciting times that lie ahead as you determine in your heart to seek only a covenant partner by engaging in *covenant dating*. Such a commitment will keep your focus on discerning who God is sending to you and the only way He wants you to receive them. It is our prayer that men and women of all ages will use this as a tool to build and maintain healthy relationships within the realm of Christianity.

Chapter 1
Why Covenant Dating

A born-again believer in Jesus Christ is already in covenant with God through Christ's sacrifice on the cross. Therefore, any single person who desires to have a marriage partner must be able to incorporate that partner into his or her relationship with Christ according to the will of God. There is only one way it can be entered into and that is by covenant. This is irrevocable and is the way marriage, or a covenant union is meant to be.

> Know ye not that ye are the temple of God,
> and *that* the Spirit of God dwelleth in you?
> 1 Cor 3:16

Because He dwells in you, you cannot make Him have a covenant with a boyfriend, a one night stand, or a common-law, live-in lover. He will not recognize these types of unions or bless them. Consequently, there can be no relationship with God apart from a covenant. Conner and Malmin assert in their book *The Covenants* that "The general purpose for a covenant is to provide a binding sense of commitment to an interpersonal relationship… and is vividly illustrated in the marriage covenant which was instituted by God to be a model of His covenants" (3). A marriage or covenant union is meant to be irrevocable except for adultery, abuse, or abandonment. This premise is further supported by Conner and Malmin who conclude that "God hates divorce because it disannuls a covenant, destroys its very purpose and does not accurately reflect the irrevocability of the covenants by which man is redeemed as reflected in Mal 2:14-16" (3). Finally, covenant dating will transform your thinking and cause you to date differently and with a greater purpose in righteousness and holiness. Moreover, it will offer you the protection God provides through your obedience to His Word.

Personal Reflection: _____

_____

_____

_____

_____

_____

_____

_____

_____

_____

Chapter 2
Biblical Sex Education 101

The word *covenant* in Scripture refers to an agreement or contract between two (or more) people or between God and people. In each case when a covenant was instituted between God and man, God was the initiator.

A. **What is a covenant?** – A contract between God and man drawn up by God and presented to man. The only thing man could do was accept or reject the proposal, but he could not change it.

B. **What is the purpose of a covenant?** – To add a binding sense of commitment to the creation of an interpersonal relationship.

The prophet Malachi admonished the people of Jerusalem because of their sinful state of relationships with one another (Mal. 2:10) and declared: "Have we not all one father? hath not one God created us? why do we deal treacherously every man against his brother, by profaning the covenant of our fathers?" During this period, men were marrying heathen women who worshipped idols, in addition to divorcing them without discretion to their alleged covenant relationships. Such annulments of marriage negated their commitment to God's standard for obedience.

God hates divorce because it annuls a covenant, destroys its very purpose, and does not accurately reflect the irrevocability of the covenants by which man is redeemed (Mal. 2:14-16).

Further Study: During Old Testament times, men had the exclusive prerogative to divorce their wives. What does "take heed to your spirit" mean in verse 16? _____

_____

_____

_____

_____

_____

Personal Reflection: _____

_____

_____

_____

_____

Let's Talk Covenant...

God chose to express His will and purpose for man through nine divine covenants although, this text focuses on the Edenic and Adamic covenants only.

A. **What are the components of a divine covenant?**
   1. Words or Promises of the Covenant
   2. Blood of the Covenant
   3. Seal of the Covenant

Any covenant is incomplete and therefore invalid without the testimony of these three things. A covenant is viewed as a life-and-death commitment, and its ratification involves bloodshed. The sacrificial blood used to make the covenant official represents the life commitment of those entering into the covenant.

B. **How is a covenantal relationship established?**
   For a covenant relationship to be established both parties must understand and fulfill their part of the covenant agreement (Gen. 17:7-18).

Further Study: There are nine biblical covenants. Name each covenant and identify the focus of the two most referenced in this text.

1. _____   4. _____   7. _____
2. _____   5. _____   8. _____
3. _____   6. _____   9. _____

       A. _____   B. _____

Personal Reflection: _____

_____

_____

_____

_____

_____

_____

_____

_____

_____

_____

Leviticus

"Leviticus was written to show Israel how to live as a priestly Kingdom and holy nation in fellowship with God. In Genesis man was ruined and Israel was born; in Exodus people were redeemed and Israel delivered; in Leviticus people were cleansed and Israel consecrated to the service of God" (Wilkinson and Boa 22).

Identify the main idea (theme) for each section of Scripture

Leviticus 15:1-14	
Leviticus 18:1-30	
Leviticus 19:1-18	
Leviticus 20:1-5 & 10-21	

We were created to have a close relationship with God,
and when fellowship is broken
we are incomplete and need restoration
according to the Life Application Study Bible, King James Version (178)

**Personal Reflection**: _____

_____

_____

_____

_____

God's Relationship to His Creation
And
His Covenant

Edenic Covenant	Adamic Covenant
• Made before the entrance of sin, involving the original man (Adam) and woman (Eve). • Revealed God's original purpose for the whole of Adam's race.	• Made after the entrance of sin with Adam and Eve, the original sinners and parents of the human race. • Involved God's judgment on sin and the coming of Messianic redemption (Gen. 3) • Provided an animal sacrifice that clothed them along with the promise that the seed of the woman would put his foot on the head of the seed of the serpent.

Note: "In every case in Scripture when a covenant was instituted between God and man, God is seen as the initiator. Man did not come to God with a proposal seeking God's approval, rather God came to man declaring His will and seeking man's adherence. A covenant is a contract between God and man drawn up by God and presented to man. Man can either accept it or reject it, but he cannot change it" (Conner & Malmin 2).

Chapter 3
Still Say No!

Failure to obey God's commandments is a result of compromising your faith to your flesh. This is how Satan seduced the first couple in Genesis. He did not tell them how it feels to fail God nor the guilt, shame, and misery they would experience as a result of their disobedience. This was experienced after the fall and failure to obey God's command.

> *A relationship with God*
> *is the most important relationship*
> *you can have.*
> *trust Him and everything*
> *will always turn out fine*

Today's moral climate in society is as much as it was in the Apostle Paul's day when he responded to Corinthian believers who questioned the culture and conduct of rampart immoral sexual practices and religious prostitution. In 1Cor. 7:1-9, Paul addresses the inquiries of the church by outlining authoritative courses of action which suggest living God's way one day at a time.

Dedicating oneself to a single individual as ascribed in Scripture will yield positive outcomes since God will show you what to do and how it should be done. Covenant dating, therefore, promotes and establishes how people of faith can honor God through their relationships.

Personal Reflection: _____

_____

_____

_____

_____

_____

_____

Chapter 4
The Sacredness of Dating

Dating for believers is meant to be a series of sacred moments. We are to use the time to grow closer together, and to understand each other and create special moments to win over the heart of the other.

Building Special Moments	
Complete the chart below, independent of the person you may be dating, listing special times that you have spent together and then compare notes.	
Special Moments With My Covenant Date	**My Covenant Date's Special Moments With Me**
1. _____ _____ _____ _____	1. _____ _____ _____ _____
2. _____ _____ _____ _____	2. _____ _____ _____ _____
3. _____ _____ _____ _____	3. _____ _____ _____ _____
4. _____ _____ _____ _____	4. _____ _____ _____ _____
5. _____ _____ _____ _____	5. _____ _____ _____ _____

Chapter 5
Who's Holding Court?

Just as we change when we are converted from sin to Christ and His righteousness, we must be converted from the ways of the world to the new life in the Kingdom of God, and we are to walk, talk, and live as lights of the world. You must also assess your spiritual walk and maturity in Christ to be a godly husband or wife someday. One must prepare to be that godly spouse according to the Scriptures.

Further Study: Covenant dating and courtship involves one man and one woman spending intentional time together getting to know each other with the expressed purpose of evaluating the other as a potential husband or wife. However, the establishment of personal goals is also an integral component of your decision making about a covenant partner and represents an opportunity to learn more about yourself. In the space provided on the next page identify one short-term (one to three years) goal and one long-term (five to seven years) goal for each of the categories below. Each should be ***SMART*** as illustrated by Sherfield and Moody:

- ***Specific***: what, when, where, and why

- ***Measurable***: concrete (quantitative vs. qualitative)

- ***Attainable***: reasonable yet challenging

- ***Relevant***: important to you and your well-being

- ***Time-bound***: realistic deadline although adaptable consistent with circumstances

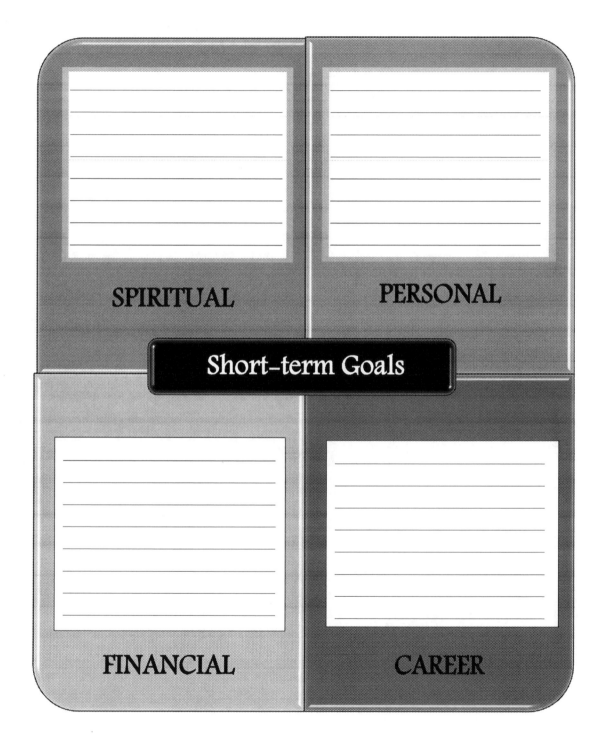

SPIRITUAL

PERSONAL

Short-term Goals

FINANCIAL

CAREER

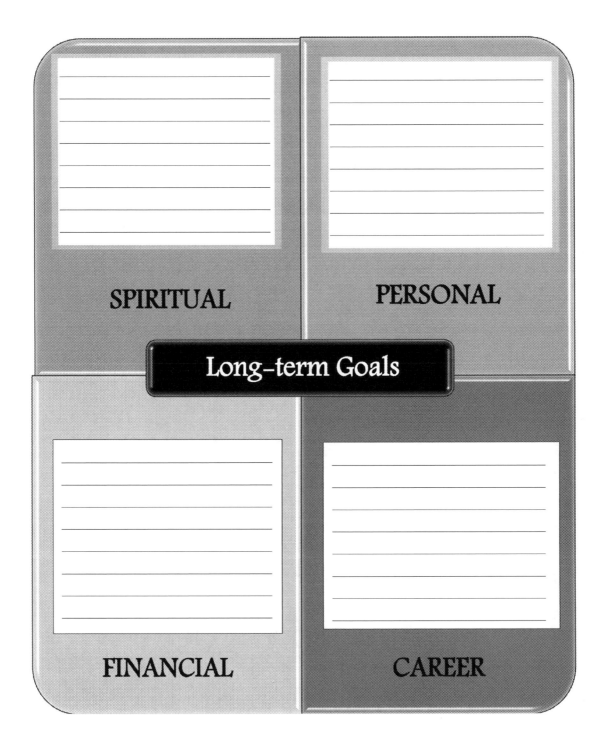

SPIRITUAL

PERSONAL

Long-term Goals

FINANCIAL

CAREER

Covenant Dating

Emotionally and physically intimate with only one member of the opposite sex... your spouse

Tends to encourage time spent in group activities or with other people the couple knows well

Approaches relationships from a perspective of ministry and service while bringing glory to God

Assumes no physical intimacy and limited emotional intimacy outside of marriage

I can do all things through Christ which strengtheneth me.
Phil.4.13

Personal Reflections: _____

_____
_____
_____
_____
_____
_____
_____
_____
_____
_____

**Finally, brethren,
whatsoever things are true,
whatsoever things are honest,
whatsoever things are just,
whatsoever things are pure,
whatsoever things are lovely,
whatsoever things are of good report;
if there be any virtue,
and if there be any praise,
think on these things.
Those things,
which ye have both learned,
and received, and heard,
and seen in me,
do: and the God of peace
shall be with you.
Phil.4:8-9**

"Lord, Prepare Me to Be a Sanctuary"

> You must assess your own
> spiritual walk and maturity in Christ
> in order to be a godly husband or wife someday.
> One must prepare to be
> that godly spouse
> according to the Scriptures.

Further Study: Identify three Gospel songs that support your understanding of covenant dating:

Song # 1 _____

Song #2 _____

Song #3 _____

Personal Reflection: Explain why the lyrics of one of the songs noted above is meaningful to you:

_____

_____

_____

_____

_____

_____

_____

_____

_____

_____

_____

Chapter 7
Does He Yada You?

The process by which Adam and Eve came to "know good and evil" is a lesson for humanity and especially for our topic of covenant dating. God said we are not to commit fornication or adultery. Fornication is premarital sex; adultery is sex with another while being married. Each represents a break in a covenant, the first to God, and the second to your spouse. Before we become covenant partners with one another, we as believers are in covenant to God through Jesus Christ our Lord.

Further Study: In the Apostle Paul's address to the church of Corinth, he says: "Know ye not that ye are the temple of God, and *that* the spirit of God dwelleth in you?" (1 Cor. 3:16). Give an example of how this still applies to covenant dating today.

_____

_____

_____

_____

_____

_____

_____

_____

_____

Personal Reflection: _____

_____

_____

_____

_____

_____

_____

_____

_____

_____

_____

_____

Sex as well as its purpose was designed by God for one male (Adam) and one female (Eve), who were told to be fruitful and multiply. Fruitful means to have sexual intimacy or the act of intercourse. The result would be to reproduce after their kind.

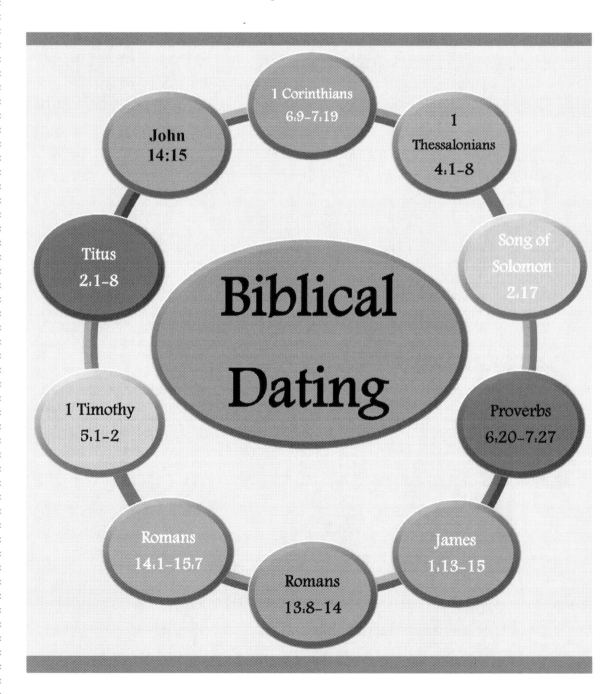

Chapter 8: The Evolution of Casual Sex

Write the corresponding Scripture noted on the previous page regarding Biblical Dating to each summary statement below

1	Favor others not self, value what's good to their souls	
2	If you love Christ, you will obey His commands (above your own desires) and live biblically	
3	Do not awaken love before it pleases – i.e., before the proper time, meaning marriage	
4	Do not defraud one another in relationships – by implying a relationship or commitment by your words or conduct that does not actually exist	
5	Young men and women should focus on self-control/godliness	
6	Love others, work for their soul's good, don't look to please self	
7	Warning to avoid sexual sin and foolish relationships	
8	Treat single women as sisters in Christ, with absolute purity	
9	The command to be pure, seriousness of sexual sin, instructions regarding marriage	
10	Temptation is to be taken very seriously	

(Refer to textbook for correct responses as needed)

With the sexual revolution, female modesty became the first casualty, and women who desired marriage lost their greatest power to hold and discipline prospective mates. They failed to realize that a woman's refusal of sexual opportunities—with hints of later gratification—is generally a necessary condition for transforming a man's lust into love.

God predetermined romantic passion when Adam and Eve were yet in His mind, and when He formed man from the dust of the ground and breathed into his nostrils the breath of life. But after the fall, man's intentions and how he would use what God had designated for him (to have one partner and produce after their kind) was polluted by the entrance of sin.

Chapter 9
Why Sex Is Not Casual

Sex is not a casual experience because:

A. Sex was never designed to be a casual or informal exercise. It is to take place within a covenant relationship only and safeguarded by all individuals as a holy gift from God.
B. It represents God and His union with His church, which He purchased with His blood.
C. The marriage covenant is a model of God's covenant with His church.

What the Bible Says About Marriage
(Life Application Study Bible)

Genesis 2:18-24	Marriage is God's idea
Genesis 24:58-60	Commitment is essential to a successful marriage
Genesis 29:10, 11	Romance is important
Jeremiah 7:34	Marriage holds times of great joy
Malachi 2: 14, 15	Marriage creates the best environment for raising children
Matthew 5:32	Unfaithfulness breaks the bond of trust, the foundation of all relationships
Matthew 19:6	Marriage is permanent
Romans 7:2, 3	Ideally, only death should dissolve a marriage
Ephesians 5:21-33	Marriage is based on the principled practice of love, not on feelings
Ephesians 5:23-32	Marriage is a living symbol of Christ and the church
Hebrews 13:4	Marriage is good and honorable

Personal Reflection: _____

_____

_____

_____

_____

_____

_____

_____

_____

Chapter 10
Oxytocin—What Turns You On

Regardless of how old you are, do not put yourself in situations where mood changes can lead to sexual activity. The human body is too vulnerable to be left to intellect and overconfidence. The road to sex, once initiated, is so strong that you cannot give any room to start and stop. We are told in Scripture to put no confidence in the flesh, your own, or anyone else's. Some of the most sincere and experienced couples have been overtaken by their emotions and feelings. The enemy has all this information and relies on the lack of knowledge and overconfidence of believers to trap them in their fleshly desires despite their spiritual commitments. Holiness and sexual purity are possible if we follow God's guidelines and spiritual precepts according to 1 Thessalonians 4:4.

That every one of you should know
how to possess his vessel in sanctification and honor.

Arousing physical touch causes our bodies to produce a powerful hormone called oxytocin. Because of the strength of this hormone's effects on our behavior, precautions must be taken to prevent us from being vulnerable to fleshly desires when out of covenant. The cycle begins with touch because:

1. Touch causes our bodies to produce the hormone oxytocin.
2. This hormone promotes a desire to touch and be touched.
3. When this hormone is released consistently at one time, its floodgates open and course through the body, causing a desire to fulfill the need to be touched—even sexually penetrated—because of the corresponding increase in testosterone production. This causes the sex drive to increase, making it extremely difficult to stop.

Spiritual steps must be implemented and practiced to help keep the flesh under subjection and have boundaries solidified by prayer, fasting, and the study of Scripture. The practice of these three disciplines can grow faith in addition to spiritual strength while developing a greater understanding of your value in Christ.

Personal Reflection: _____

_____

_____

_____

Chapter 11
Celibacy, the Next Best Gift

Spiritual virginity is just as important as physical virginity when the latter is no longer an option. This means that abstinence is practiced throughout your time of dating and courting to ascertain who will be the right choice for a priest, prayer partner, husband, father, and friend, or helpmeet, prayer partner, wife, mother, and caregiver.

There are some who had no say in the loss of their virginity, such as victims of rape and molestation, but others gave away this onetime gift willingly in ignorance of the biblical order. It is not too late to gain back spiritually what you lost physically. If you did know better and just wanted to experiment with your sexuality you can repent and ask the Lord's forgiveness; He is quick to forgive and cleanse. While this will not produce a new hymen to be broken, it will produce a new mindset, for God's cleansing is so good it is as though the event never happened.

But celibacy is suggested for a reason (until a covenant union of marriage has taken place), and the season lasts until there is a candidate who serves the same God as you and believes His Word like you and has had time to get to know you – the true inner you, not the physical sexual you. It is usually done backward: the attraction draws you together and lust starts to take hold, and before you can work on the most important details you discover each other sexually only to find out later you are not compatible.

When we act on the promises of God by saving our sexuality for covenantal relationships -- either marriage or celibacy -- our bodies radiate with the holiness of love, both here and now, and more profoundly in the world to come.

Personal Reflection: _____

_____

_____

_____

_____

_____

_____

_____

_____

_____

_____

Chapter 12
Your Worst Move

When we remain sexually abstinent before marriage and faithful within marriage, we are not simply saying no to sex but rather yes to God's unique plan.

Like married people, singles are called to steward their sexuality as a gift from God. They do so through faithful devotion to Christ. When they forego or await the intimacies of marriage they affirm the exclusive covenantal relationship of marriage and all it symbolizes. Celibacy is a worthy state for mature men and women. God's mortal standards are meant for ultimate freedom and protection in sexual expression.

According to Glenn T. Stanton author of *The Ring Makes All the Difference: The Hidden Consequences of Cohabitation and the Strong Benefits of Marriage*, a woman who cohabitates before marriage will increase her likelihood of getting a husband who exhibits the behaviors illustrated below:

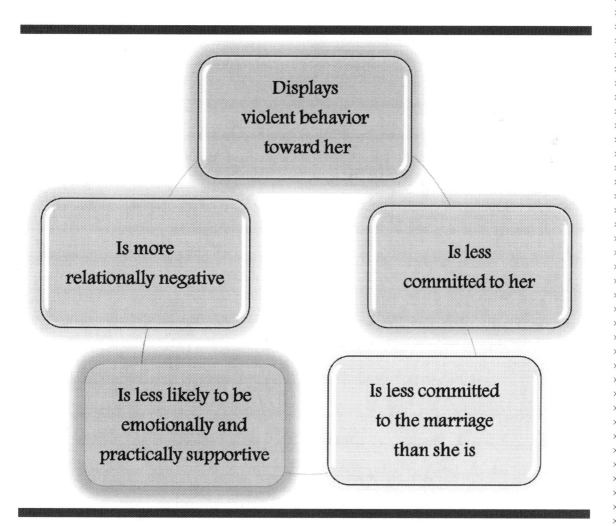

Chapter 13
Let's Set Some Boundaries

Boundaries are designed to protect and define an individual. Dating is a time to find out if a person is suitable for courtship, and courtship is done in preparation for a covenant commitment. Choosing a lifelong covenant partner is the most important decision you will make after you decide to make Jesus Christ your Lord and Savior. It will take time to know whether an individual is suitable as a covenant partner. While you are getting to know someone who has the potential to become your covenant partner, safeguards must remain in place—in the form of boundaries.

<u>Practical Advice on Dating</u>
No Man's Concubine by Evangelist Beverly D. Allen

- Keep your dates public. Be in an open surrounding and yet a quiet setting where you can talk and get to know one another.
- Before the date, prepare what will make for a good conversation.
- Plan what you will wear ahead of time. This will help you determine the appropriate attire for this occasion.
- When you learn where you are going, always let someone know where and with whom you are going. Carry a cell phone should plans change at the last minute.
- Become familiar with new standards in etiquette and table manners.
- Have a set time to be home. The purpose of dating is to collect information to help you determine if there is potential for furthering the relationship.
- If you sincerely pass the first three or four dates and see that there is a mutual attraction, and you plan to continue seeing each other, work out some boundaries that you both agree on as Christians.
- As mature Christian adults, sit down together and plan how to pray to keep the enemy of lust from steering this potential relationship off course.
- If you both live alone, do not entertain at either of your apartments if there are no other Christian couples present. And they should leave when you leave and stay while you are there.
- Whenever you start to show affection, you move to a new level and it is hard to return to just what was done before that. Remember that nothing is hidden from God.
- At this point, dating which has moved to courtship cannot be endless. There should be planning for the wedding and preparation, not just for a ceremony, but also for a life together.
- Pray together often and encourage each other through the Word of God.

God gave specific roles to both the man and woman, Adam and Eve. Adam would have a threefold responsibility that would imitate God's responsibility for His creation. Jehovah-Jireh (the Lord who provides) governs as Father, guides as the Son, and guards as the Holy Spirit. This breaks down as a threefold responsibility to direct, protect, and correct. God modeled for Adam his responsibility as His earthly representative to be an example to all men.

You cannot settle for being unevenly yoked, for what hath light in common with darkness? The truth is there may be some things the two of you have in common, but not the most important thing—Christ.

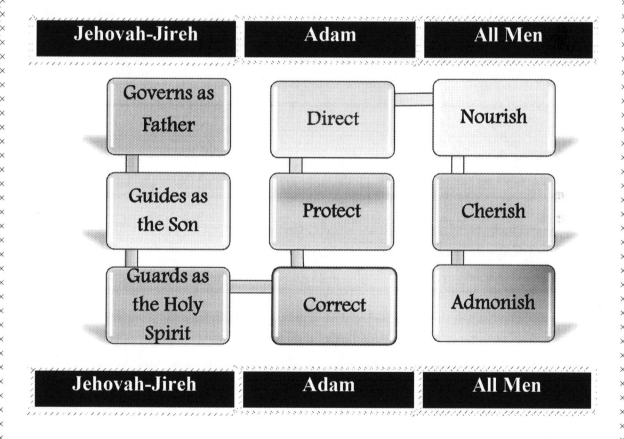

Chapter 15
Same-Sex and the Covenant

If a man lies with a man as one lies with a woman,
both of them have done what is detestable.
Leviticus 20:13

Any relationship outside of God's design sexually is perverted, disobedient, and not sanctioned by Him. The same gender may have unions in which they have sex and call it marriage, but it will never be recognized as a biblical covenant by God.

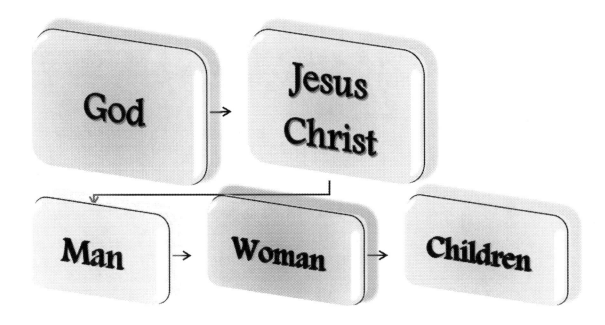

The male and female were designed for procreation and intimacy with each other. When they become one, it is the most spiritual and holy act they can commit with each other, and when permitted they bear the fruit of children from this union which God Himself sanctions

Personal Reflection: _____

_____

_____

_____

_____

_____

_____

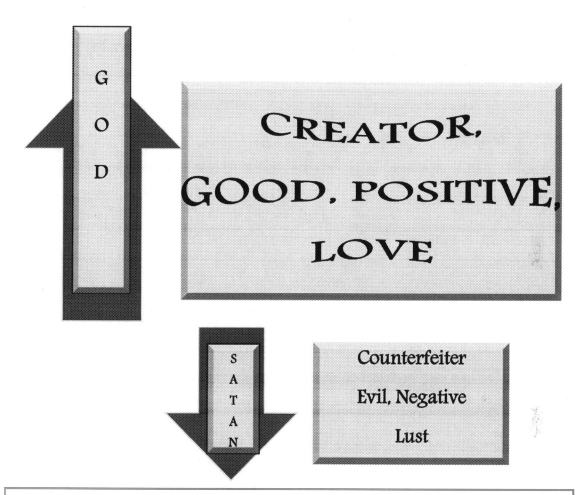

Love	Lust
Love desires to benefit others at the expense of self because love desires to give.	***Lust*** desires to benefit them self at the expense of others because lust desires to get.

Directions: Identify two behaviors you need to change and how you will accomplish them:

Behavior to change	How to accomplish behavioral change

Conclusion

Choosing a covenant partner requires help from the all-knowing, all-powerful God, our Father and Lord. Abiding in His Word and following His plan is best for all believers. Selecting your most intimate partner in life and committing to them is a serious matter. Let's change the way things are going, away from the order of God, back to His plan and order, which begins with each believer.

Whenever you begin anew to conduct yourself in godly relationships that glorify God and keep yourself emotionally and spiritually safe, the peace of God that passes all understanding will comfort your heart and safeguard your body. Walk with the Lord daily and seek His counsel; be filled with the Spirit of God that you may hear Him speaking to your spirit from within, guiding your steps. Trust Him with all your heart. He will not break it, and He will not send someone to you who will, but one who will love you as Christ loves the church, His bride!

Appendix 1-A
Covenant Dating
Discussion/Study Questions

1. ***What is the purpose of a covenant? (Ch. 2)***

   _____

   _____

   _____

2. ***What happens to those who enter into covenant? (Ch. 2)***

   _____

   _____

   _____

3. ***Why does God hate divorce? (Ch. 2)***

   _____

   _____

   _____

4. ***What does the word covenant signify? (Ch. 2)***

   _____

   _____

   _____

5. ***When a covenant was instituted between God and man, who was the initiator? Explain. (Ch. 2)***

   _____

   _____

   _____

6. ***What are the three (3) parts of the divine covenant? (Ch. 2)***

   _____

   _____

   _____

7. ***Is a covenant complete if one or two of these parts are missing? (Ch. 2)***

   _____

   _____

   _____

8. *What does each member of the triune Godhead represent in the covenant agreement?* *(Ch. 2)*

_____

_____

_____

9. *What does the sacrificial blood used in the covenant represent? Explain. (Ch. 2)*

_____

_____

_____

10. *Who offered up the sacrifice? (Ch. 2)*

_____

_____

_____

11. *What three things were required in a "blood" covenant? (Ch. 2)*

_____

_____

_____

12. *According to the Old Testament Scriptures, how was a sacrifice offered? (Ch. 2)*

_____

_____

_____

13. *What was the purpose of the seal? (Ch. 2)*

_____

_____

_____

14. *What is the Edenic covenant? (Ch. 2)*

_____

_____

_____

15. *What are the necessary covenant components within the Edenic covenant? (Ch. 2)*

_____

_____

_____

16. *What was Satan's aim in the Edenic covenant? (Ch. 2)*

_____

_____

_____

17. *What were the results of Adam and Eve's act of disobedience (Ch.2)*

_____

_____

_____

18. *What were the three necessary elements in God's covenant with man? Explain each element. (Ch. 2)*

_____

_____

_____

19. *Explain how God designed man and woman to provide the three necessary components of a covenant? (Ch. 2)*

_____

_____

_____

20. *What do the three necessary components—words, blood, and seal—of the covenant require? (Ch. 2)*

_____

_____

_____

21. *What covenant necessities found in the Edenic and Adamic covenants, and the covenant made with Abraham, have in common with the marriage covenant? Name them. (Ch. 2)*

_____

_____

_____

22. *What do the three necessary components—words, blood, and seal—of the covenant require? (Ch. 2)*

_____

_____

_____

23. *How do you practice celibacy? (Ch. 3)*

_____

_____

_____

24. *What is the answer to avoiding sexual immorality according to 1 Corinthians 7:1-3? (Ch. 3)*

_____

_____

_____

25. *How should believers view dating? (Ch. 4)*

_____

_____

_____

26. *What is the word in Genesis used to indicate a knowledge of information and facts about a person and even intimacy of sexual intercourse? (Ch. 7)*

_____

_____

_____

27. *Knowing implies what where yada is used in Genesis 3:5, 22, and Deuteronomy 1:39? (Ch. 7)*

_____

_____

_____

28. *Give at least four scriptures that support biblical dating. (Ch. 8)*

_____

_____

_____

29. *What does 1 Corinthians 7:3 teach? (Ch. 9)*

_____

_____

_____

30. *Which hormone plays a significant role in our sexuality? (Ch. 10)*

_____

_____

_____

31. *Oxytocin increases the levels of _____, the sex hormone in the woman. (Ch. 10)*

32. *What season is a time to cultivate patience, especially in our sexuality? (Ch. 11)*

_____

_____

_____

33. *Name one of the problems that exists during singleness (Ch. 11)*

_____

_____

_____

34. *Cohabitation is a counterfeit relationship of what true, authentic, and committed relationship? (Ch. 12)*

_____

35. *Boundaries are the key to keeping your soul _____, _____, and _____. (Ch. 13)*

36. *Dating is a time to find out what? (Ch. 13)*

_____

_____

_____

37. *In which scripture does Paul speak about dishonorable passions? (Ch. 14)*

_____

38. *What does due penalty in Romans 1:27 refer to? (Ch. 14)*

_____

_____

_____

39. *How does Adam represent God in marriage? (Ch. 14)*

_____

_____

_____

40. *How would all men imitate Adam and God? (Ch. 14)*

_____

_____

_____

41. *What is the first thing a potential mate must-have? (Ch. 14)*

_____

_____

_____

42. *Write the scripture in the OT that gives God's command against same-sex relationships. (Ch. 15)*

_____

43. *What else changes when you change your mind? (Ch. 16)*

_____

_____

_____

44. *Write a scripture that speaks about changing one's mind. (Ch. 16)*

_____

_____

_____

45. *Where do our battles take place first? (Ch. 16)*

_____

_____

_____

46. *Name two groups of emotions. (Ch. 16)*

_____

_____

_____

47. *Fear and faith are more than just emotions. Explain. (Ch. 16)*

_____

_____

_____

48. *How do our emotions affect us? (Ch. 16)*

_____

_____

_____

49. *Why do we need to control our emotions? (Ch. 16)*

_____

_____

_____

50. *Complete this sentence:* God our Father wants us to prosper in every area of our lives, especially _____ in our covenant dating choices. *(Ch. 16)*

Appendix 1-B

Covenant Dating
Answers for Discussion/Study Questions

1. ***What is the purpose of a covenant? (Ch. 2)***
   - To provide a binding sense of commitment to an interpersonal relationship

2. ***What happens to those who enter into covenant? (Ch. 2)***
   - They obligate themselves to that relationship and provide it with a strong sense of security.

3. ***Why does God hate divorce? (Ch. 2)***
   - Because it annuls a covenant, destroys its very purpose, and does not accurately reflect the irrevocability of the covenants by which man is redeemed (Mal. 2:14-16).

4. ***What does the word* covenant *signify? (Ch. 2)***
   - It signifies a mutual understanding between two or more parties, each binding himself or herself to fulfill specified obligations; a legal contract; a binding agreement; a written agreement.

5. ***When a covenant was instituted between God and man, who was the initiator? Please explain. (Ch. 2)***
   - God was the initiator. The man did not come to God with a proposal seeking His approval; rather God came to man declaring His will and seeking man's adherence.

6. ***What are the three (3) parts of the divine covenant? (Ch. 2)***
   a. Word/Promise
   b. Blood
   c. Seal

7. ***Is a covenant complete if one or two of these parts are missing? (Ch. 2)***
   - No, they must all be present within the covenant.

8. ***What does each member of the triune Godhead represent in the covenant agreement? (Ch. 2)***
   - The Father is the originator and initiator.
   - The Son is the mediator and ratifier.
   - The Holy Spirit is the executor (the seal is given by His work in us).

9. ***What does the sacrificial blood used in the covenant represent? Explain. (Ch. 2)***
   - The life commitment of those entering into the covenant. A covenant is viewed as a life-and-death commitment; the ratification of it involves bloodshed.

10. ***Who offered up the sacrifice? (Ch. 2)***
    - A priest. It was necessary to offer the sacrifice in a sanctuary, a sacred place where the priest could function.

11. ***What three things were required in a "blood" covenant? (Ch. 2)***
    a. Sacrifice
    b. Priest
    c. Sanctuary

12. ***According to the Old Testament Scriptures, how was a sacrifice offered? (Ch. 2)***
    - It mandated a sacrificer or the mediator officiating the covenant ratification ceremony.

13. ***What was the purpose of the seal? (Ch. 2)***
    - It provided an ongoing tangible witness to the veracity of the covenant. Proof!

14. ***What is the Edenic covenant? (Ch. 2)***
    - It is the covenant God made in the Garden with Adam and Eve before the fall which expressed His purpose in creation.

15. ***What are the six necessary components within the Edenic covenant? (Ch. 2)***
    - Words/Promises
    - Terms
    - Blood
    - Mediator
    - Place/Sanctuary
    - Seal/Sign

16. ***What tree was Adam removed from when he disobeyed God's command? (Ch. 2)***
    - The tree of life.

17. ***What was Satan's aim in the Edenic covenant? (Ch. 2)***
    - He aimed to break the covenantal relationship between the Creator and the creature by deceiving man into violating the covenant.

18. ***What were the results of Adam and Eve's act of disobedience? (Ch. 2)***
    - Man's covenantal relationship with God and his character were corrupted by the entrance of sin and death.

19. ***What were the three necessary elements in God's covenant with man? Explain each element. (Ch. 2)***
    a. <u>***Words/Promises***</u> – Gen. 3:15 – The Seed of the woman would bruise the serpent's head.
    b. <u>***Blood***</u> – God judged self-righteousness to be insufficient (Isa. 64:6). Neither fig leaves nor anything else man attempts to do will ever make him right before God. Therefore a substitutionary sacrifice was needed.
    c. <u>***Mediator***</u> – God Himself acted as the mediator, the priest of this covenant (p. 13). As the Lord God demonstrated His priesthood on Adam's behalf, He set an example for Adam to follow in being the priest of his household.

20. ***Explain how God designed man and woman to provide the three necessary components of a covenant? (Ch. 2)***
    - Male and female in the ability to become one flesh were designed anatomically for the act of sexual intercourse. This is the only relationship of a blood covenant fulfilling God's original intent for husband and wife.

21. ***What do the three necessary components—words, blood, and seal—of the covenant require? (Ch. 2)***
    - A mediator and a place

22. ***What covenant necessities found in the Edenic and Adamic covenants, and the covenant made with Abraham, have in common with the marriage covenant? Name them. (Ch. 2)***
    - Words or Promises
    - Blood
    - Seal
    - Mediator/Priest
    - A Place/Sanctuary

23. ***How do you practice celibacy? (Ch. 3)***
    - The Scriptures teach in Romans 13:14, "make no provision for the flesh." This means do not put yourself in situations that make it easy to comply with your fleshly desires. For if you do, the flesh will take control.

24. ***What is the answer to avoiding sexual immorality according to 1 Corinthians 7:1-3? (Ch. 3)***
    - Let each man have his own wife and let each woman have her own husband.

25. ***How should believers view dating? (Ch. 4)***
    - As sacred moments that make God a part of the time spent together. This will help the believer conduct each date with God's awareness.

26. ***What is the word in Genesis used to indicate a knowledge of information and facts about a person and even intimacy of sexual intercourse? (Ch. 7)***
    - Yada.

27. ***Knowing implies what where yada is used in Genesis 3:5, 22, and Deuteronomy 1:39? (Ch. 7)***
    - The process by which one recognizes, classifies, and systematizes the data gained from experience. The phrase in these scriptures focuses on the process of making moral distinctions and coming to conclusions about what is good and what is evil.

28. ***Give at least four scriptures that support biblical dating. (Ch. 8)***
    - 1 Corinthians 6:9 – 7:19, Titus 2:1 – 829, Proverbs 6:20 – 7:27, Song 2:17. Chemical processes take place in our bodies that activate three mating drives. What are they? (p. 52) Lust, romantic attraction, and attachment.

29. ***What does 1 Corinthians 7:3 teach? (Ch. 9)***
    - The husband should fulfill his marital duty to his wife and likewise the wife to her husband. The wife's body belongs to her husband and the husband's body likewise belongs to the wife.

30. ***Which hormone plays a significant role in our sexuality? (Ch. 10)***
    - Oxytocin

31. ***Oxytocin increases the levels of _____, the sex hormone in the woman. (Ch. 10)***
    - Testosterone

32. ***What season is a time to cultivate patience, especially in our sexuality? (Ch. 11)***
    - Celibacy

33. *Name one of the problems that exists during singleness. (Ch. 11)*
   - Our bodies are ready for sexual intimacy long before we have met the criteria for marriage.

34. *Cohabitation is a counterfeit relationship of what true, authentic, and committed relationship? (Ch. 12)*
   - Marriage

35. *Boundaries are the key to keeping your soul _____, _____, and _____. (Ch. 13)*
   - Safe, protected, and growing

36. *Dating is a time to find out what? (Ch. 13)*
   - If an individual is suitable for courtship and courtship in preparation for a covenant.

37. *In which scripture does Paul speak about dishonorable passions? (Ch. 14)*
   - Romans 1:26-27

38. *What does due penalty in Romans 1:27 refer to? (Ch. 14)*
   - It refers to a penalty that is appropriate to the wrong committed.

39. *How does Adam represent God in marriage? (Ch. 14)*
   - Adam would represent God because his responsibility also was to direct, protect, and correct.

40. *How would all men imitate Adam and God? (Ch. 14)*
   - To nourish, cherish, and admonish all of humanity by bringing forth after their kind. Nourish as a provider, cherish his gift of family and role of life-giver, and admonish others to follow God and obey His order and Word.

41. *What is the first thing a potential mate must-have? (Ch. 14)*
   - He or she must have a covenant relationship with the Lord and Savior Jesus Christ.

42. *Give the scripture in the OT that gives God's command against same-sex relationships. (Ch. 15)*
   - Leviticus 18:22 – Do not lie with a man as one lies with a woman; that is detestable. Also, Leviticus 20:13 – If a man lies with a man as one lies with a woman both of them have done what is detestable.

43. *What else changes when you change your mind? (Ch. 16)*
   - You change your life, your choices, and your behavior.

44. *Give a scripture that speaks about changing one's mind. (Ch. 16)*
   - Romans 12:2 – Be ye transformed by the renewing of your mind.

45. *Where do our battles take place first? (Ch. 16)*
   - In the mind.

46. *Name two groups of emotions. (Ch. 16)*
   - Positive faith-based emotions and negative fear-based emotions.

47. *Fear and faith are more than just emotions. Explain. (Ch. 16)*
   - They are spiritual forces with chemical and electrical representation in the body.

48. *How do our emotions affect us? (Ch. 16)*
   - Every emotion results in an attitude, which is a state of mind that produces a reaction, which in turn produces a resultant behavior.

49. *Why do we need to control our emotions? (Ch. 16)*
   - We need to control our emotions because of the impact they have on our bodies and mind.

50. *Complete this sentence. (Ch. 16)*
   - God our Father wants us to prosper in every area of our life, especially _____ in our covenant partnership choices.

Appendix 2
Covenant Dating Agreement

Dating is a God-focused, mutually edifying relationship that has as its intentional goal the glorification of God through biblical marriage.

1. ***We agree and promise to adhere to the above definition of dating, and in our relationship we covenant to:***

   A. Stay focused (*Heb. 12:2, 2 Cor. 4:18, Matt. 22:37*)

   B. Be mutually edifying (*Rom. 4:19, 1 Thess. 5:11*)

   C. Make the goal of our relationship the glorification of God (*1 Cor. 10:31*) through biblical marriage (*Gen. 2:24, Eph. 5:22-33*)

   D. If we disagree with the definition of dating, the areas we disagree on are:

   a. Man

   _____

   _____

   _____

   b. Woman

   _____

   _____

   _____

   c. Can this be resolved in the context of our relationship? How?

   _____

   _____

   _____

2. ***We agree that we will spend time together to:***

   a. Get to know each other spiritually, personally, and relationally

   b. Enjoy each other's presence

   c. Figure out if it is God's will that we get married

3. ***We will set the following boundaries during our time together:***

   a. The amount of time spent together will not be so much as to encourage us to be "one-flesh" (Genesis 2:24) as if we were married

b. We will allow and encourage each other to do the following faithfully, even if it means we will spend less time together
   1. Attend Sunday morning worship service
   2. Attend a discipleship group
   3. Serve in a ministry
   4. Practice quiet time
c. The average amount of time we will together each week is ideally:_____
d. We will set not spend more than _____ together each week

4. ***We will set the following boundaries to maintain and encourage our physical purity:***
   a. We will be obedient to Song of Solomon 2:7, 3:5, 8:4, and not "arouse or awaken love until it so desires."
   b. We will not have sexual intercourse, do anything that looks or feels like sexual intercourse, or do anything that leads to either of the above.

---

1. We acknowledge that as individuals certain things "arouse or awaken love" for one but not the other. Because of that, we will honor the weaker brother or sister (1 Cor. 8:9).

2. Specifically, we WILL/will NOT do the following:

	Proposed Items of Agreement	Will	Will Not
1	Kiss (a peck on the cheek)		
2	Kiss (a peck on the lips)		
3	Kiss (a longer kiss on the lips)		
4	Kiss (a lingering kiss on the lips)		
5	Kiss (French)		
6	Kiss (other than the above)		
7	Touch (hold – hands)		
8	Touch (a hug – side)		
9	Touch (a hug – front)		
10	Touch (a hug - behind)		
11	Touch (caress any part of the body)		

5. ***We will actively and honestly pursue regular accountability***
   a. ***Relational Accountability*** – we will talk together and with wise Christian friends regularly about the condition and future of our relationship (James 5:16).

       1. Who (Man) _____

       2. Who (Woman) _____

       3. How often? _____

  b. ***Spiritual Accountability*** – we will meet regularly with our pastor/spiritual mentor to discuss the condition and future of our relationship (Heb. 13:17).

       1. Who (Man) _____

       2. Who (Woman) _____

       3. How often? _____

  c. ***Parental Accountability*** – we will consult our parents on the condition and future of our relationship (Eph. 6:4).

       1. When? _____

       2. How often? _____

  d. ***Absolute Accountability*** – we will seek God together about the condition and future of our relationship and confess our sins quickly (Rom. 3:9).

6. ***We agree to end the relationship in the case of any of the following:***
   a. When sinful patterns start to be formed and reinforced
   b. When either or both of us continually dishonor set boundaries
   c. When either or both of us start and continue to desire the other more than God
   d. When either or both of us decide that the other is not the person we want to marry

7. ***We agree to end the relationship in a loving, healthy, and biblical way (Eph. 4:15, 2 Tim. 1:7.)***
   How would we like the other to break up with us if it comes up?

   _____

   _____

   _____

   _____

Man – I have read and agree to the above and covenant to honor the things noted herein.

  Name: _____ Date: _____

Woman – I have read and agree to the above and covenant to honor the things noted herein.

  Name: _____ Date: _____

Works Cited

Allen, Beverly. *Covenant Dating.* WestBow Press, 2012.

Allen, Beverly. *No Man's Concubine.* Xulon Press, 2004.

Conner, Kevin, and Ken Malmin. "The Covenants." *The Covenants*, Portland, Oregon, City Bible Publishing, 1997.

KJV Life Application Study Bible, Second Edition. Tyndale House Publishers, Inc., 1997.

Moody, Patricia, and Sherfield, Robert. "Creating Success, Guiding Change, and Setting Goals." *Cornerstones for Community College Success (2nd Edition)*, 2nd ed., Pearson, 2013, pp. 21–22.

Stanton, Glenn. *The Ring Makes All the Difference: The Hidden Consequences of Cohabitation and the Strong Benefits of Marriage.* New, Moody Publishers, 2011.

Wilkinson, Bruce, and Kenneth Boa. *Talk Thru the Bible.* T. Nelson, 1983.

Printed in the United States
By Bookmasters